Love Lessons

D'Shan Berry

BookLeaf
Publishing

India | USA | UK

Presentation by *BookLeaf Publishing*

Web: www.bookleafpub.com

E-mail: info@bookleafpub.com

ISBN: 9789367396261

First edition 2024

Love Lessons

Love does no wrong to a neighbor;
Is the fulfillment of the Law.
Love sacrifices its comforts,
And forgives where it finds a flaw.

Love is not jealous or boastful.
Instead, love is patient and kind.
Love isn't easily angered,
But real love can feel hard to find.

Love detests lies, which are evil
Rejoicing in things that are true.
Love endures for eternity,
Sheltering hope for me and you.

Trauma Class

Who would I be without trauma?
Perchance happier, but less wise;
Less needy of medications,
But less in tune with others' cries.

I wouldn't trade my compassion
In order to lessen my pain.
I've learned more of love from my suff'ring
Than I could otherwise attain.

Empathy — fruit of our sorrows,
Tenderness towards people's grief;
The capacity to offer
Sacred silence, love, and relief.

So, yes, my trauma has changed me,
For the better and for the worse,
But post-traumatic growth exists;
Trauma needn't remain a curse.

Eclipse

As the days grow darker, so do I.
The barren trees an echo of my soul;
The colder air deflates my heart with sighs;
My body aching, longing to be whole.

I feel like I've become a dandelion,
A careless wish could scatter me away.
I've never felt so close to almost dyin',
But I've made up my mind I'm gonna stay.

But, these dark days won't get the best of me,
'Cause I've survived a dozen times before.
In the midst of this eclipse, it's hard to see,
But I have hope that Love has more in store.

The inky weight invades my weary heart
Through cracks and fissures carved out long
ago.
It pulls me down, but soon enough, I'll start
The journey back to light and life, I know.

But, these dark days won't get the best of me,

'Cause I've survived a dozen times before.
In the midst of this eclipse, it's hard to see,
But I have hope that Love has more in store.

Yeah, I have hope that Love has more in store.

Hospital

The constant hum and wheeze of ventilation,
The distant dinging bell of some alarm,
The antiseptic smell throughout the hallways,
The scratchy blanket that can't keep me warm.

The thought of losing you is overwhelming.
The burden on my heart — too much to bear.
The only thing I hope is that it's painless
The last thing that you know— how much I
care.

This Is Love

I tried so hard to keep up my defenses
Built barricades around my heart for years
But you broke through and shattered my
pretenses
Undaunted by my questions and my fears

And this is love, that you would sit with me
While I unearth the landmines of my youth.
You patiently disarm me, one by one.
You're unafraid and kill the lies with truth.

Let All Your Shame Die On The Cross

Let all your shame die on the cross,
For Jesus bore it, there.
Naked, He hung, extending grace;
There's none He cannot spare.

No spot's so dark He cannot cleanse,
Regardless of its source.
His love redeems all kinds of pain;
Compassion is His course.

Love casts out fear; truth sets you free.
Your past can't hurt you now.
Speak boldly of your life in Him;
Ask, and He'll show you how.

Griever's Lament

My heart's become an empty shell,
Receptacle for grief.
Your absence fills up everything.
I fear there's no relief.

Losing you was devastating;
A wound so hard to heal.
Ever slowly, time inches by;
Not changing how I feel.

Time, alone, cannot bring comfort,
For I need Heaven's peace.
Only as I draw near to God,
Will I find my release.

He is bigger than my sorrow;
Can handle all my pain.
With His help, I trust that, someday,
I'll learn to live again.

Dissociation

I curl in on myself,
an armadillo girl.
My soul's abatement now
a reflex - an instinct
acquired in my youth.
If I shrink small enough,
perhaps I can escape
the pain, the fear,
his hands' betrayal
of my skin.

Exultation

Ransomed captive, free at last,
Bound no longer by my past.
I'm forgiven, made complete,
By God's grace and mercy, sweet;

Not alone to bear my pain;
Suffering, not done in vain.
Hope secured by Love divine,
Peace lives in this heart of mine.

Joy beyond the end of days,
Friend to guide me on the way,
Savior of my soul, my King,
Carry me through everything.

You took my heart in Your hand;
Pulled it from the deep quicksand.
You, alone, have rescued me;
You, alone, are all I need.

Praise the Lord, who saved my soul!
Praise the Love, which made me whole!
Praise to Him on heaven's throne,
Who also makes my heart His home!

Missing You (For Meghan)

The guitar you said you'd teach me
Lies lonely in my room.
I can't bring myself to touch it
My heart is out of tune.

You left no note explaining why.
You offered no farewell.
For me, the days since then have been
A quiet tour through hell.

Missing you is like breathing,
I do it every day;
Wondering what I could've done
That would've made you stay.

Tears erode the pain a little,
But can't erase the grief.
When I see your face in Heaven,
I'll finally know relief.

One day, I may, at long last, learn
To play that old guitar.
For now, it just reminds my heart
How dear to me you are.

Missing you is like breathing,
I do it every day;
Wondering what I could've done
That would've made you stay.

Solstice Advent

The longest night nears to a close —
The Son will be here soon,
To drive the darkness from our hearts.
His love shines like the noon.

The darkness cannot comprehend
The Light in all His glory.
He came; He died; He rose again,
Remains the greatest story.

Remodeling

I'm trying to become myself
Through layers of facade;
I've whitewashed my soul for ages,
Even hiding from God.

Believing I'm too terrible,
Consumed with guilt and shame;
I've covered up myself in lies,
My fawn response to blame.

Thinking safety laid in pleasing,
I folded myself small;
Becoming like a chameleon,
So I could blend with all.

It makes knowing myself alien—
A language strange and new.
Standing on this foreign surface,
I don't know what to do.

New horizons bring new stories,
And dawn comes from each night;
Every day—filled up with pages
Which I have yet to write.

Not a Burden

You are not a heavy burden,
Borne with regret or pain.
You are not the things that haunt you,
That once filled you with shame.

Don't believe the lies life's told you;
God takes us as we come,
And there is no condemnation
Once we accept His Son.

And His truth is like an anchor
Amidst the stormy seas.
Our feelings may around us swirl,
But His truth sets us free.

Before and After

Is this what life was like before I met you?
Cold, and dark, and grey, and small, and bare.
For, since you've gone, I'm only left to wander
To and fro while reeling from despair.

The ache of missing you is ever-present
It smolders like an ember in my heart
I feel I have become a dandelion,
As if one wish could scatter me apart.

I miss you like the burning of my lungs,
Deprived of breath and yearning to inhale.
I miss you like the tide would miss the moon,
Like my red-headed skin would miss its pale.

Internal Hemorrhaging

With the corners of my mouth upturned,
On the outside, I look fine.
I echo all their "how are yous,"
But don't actually reply.

I mimic the expressions
Of emotions I can't feel.
Hope and joy have vanished.
Pain is all that's real.

Anguish, like an aneurysm,
Has ruptured deep inside,
And no one knows I'm dying
From these inward wounds I hide.

Outlet

I want to rend my flesh in grief,
Make visible my pain.
My sorrow knows of no relief,
Can see no earthly gain.

Instead of putting blade to skin,
I'll let this ballpoint bleed,
In hopes that putting hand to pen
Will fill this aching need.

My thoughts escape through inky lines,
My spirit to console.
The pressures of the day's confines
Are too much for my soul.

When tears won't come, the words will rise,
Outlet for my sorrow;
Transforming all my weary sighs
To hope which I can borrow.

On the Anniversary of the Last Time I Self-injured

Today makes twenty years
Since razors sliced my skin,
Seeking peace from sorrow
I hid and held within.

The story of my scars
I never used to share.
Shame still kept me silent,
Afraid no one would care.

Now, I tell it humbly,
In hopes to help someone;
To say, 'You're not alone,
This can be overcome.'

Poem From My Inner Child

There's salt-rings on my pillowcase
From crying lonely tears;
Evaporated pools of pain,
Encircled by my fears.

I grieve my lost sense of safety,
Taken from me so young.
It broke my sense of the future,
Thwarted what I'd become.

Reaching out and finding nothing,
I learned it hurts to try,
And so, I gave up long ago.
Now, I just ache and cry.

From Wound To Wonder

Wound is the root word of wonder —
Opening to the world.
Our wounds can also be doorways,
And through them, hope unfurled.

Letting the chinks in our armor
Be seen by other eyes,
Takes a certain kind of courage.
It's easier to hide.

But I know vulnerability
Creates a special link.
Matching struggles, scars, and stories,
Can put people in sync.

Wounds can lend more understanding
Between both friend and foe.
We all have our difficulties,
We should all let them show.

Tears in a Bottle

He captures my tears in a bottle,
Consecrating my pain.
Every sorrow that haunts me,
Made holy, not profane.

My suffering — not for nothing,
But working for my good;
My broken heart — not unwelcome,
But wanted, understood.

He said that He is near to us,
The brokenhearted crowd,
Poor in spirit, or facing grief —
Acquainted with death's shroud.

He, too, once begged the cup could pass,
The anguish not to bear,
But, for the joy of knowing us,
He died, our souls to spare.

So, it's not from a distance that
He comforts those who hurt
But rather from experience
In his time on this dirt.

Place your pain in His nail-scarred hands,
They're big enough by far,
And He already knows your heart;
Just tell Him where you are.

Last Word Spoken

I've wasted too much time on band-aids too
small for my soul.
These gaping wounds need surgery if I'm to be
made whole.

I've found temporary cures at best, never lasting
long,
But I need more than duct tape to fix everything
that's wrong.

So, wrap Your nail-pierced hands around my
heart,
Piecing back together every part
of me.
Replace what's lost.
Restore what's broken.
Don't let sorrow be
The last word spoken.

I turn to the Great Physician, who, with Your
gentle touch,
Can bind up all the shattered fragments that hurt
me so much.

Transfuse to me Your peace and mercy, fill me
up with You.
Revive my weary, broken spirit, carry my soul
through.

So, wrap Your nail-pierced hands around my
heart,
Piecing back together every part
of me.
Replace what's lost.
Restore what's broken.
Don't let sorrow be
The last word spoken.

You came to set the captive free, to heal from
inside out.
Give me faith to believe that truth; please, rescue
me from doubt.

www.ingramcontent.com/pod-product-compliance
Lightning Source LLC
Chambersburg PA
CBHW071249140726
47996CB00007B/2817